j398.6 Sterne, Noelle
ST
Tyrannosaurus
wrecks

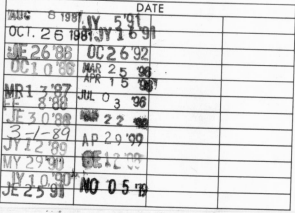

DATE			
AUG 8 198?	JY 5 '91		
OCT. 26 1981	JY 16 91		
JE 26 '86	OC 26 '92		
OC 10 '86	MAR 2 5 '96		
	APR 1 5 '9?		
MR 13 '87	JUL 0 3 '96		
FE 8 '88			
JE 30 '88	MR 22 9?		
3-1-89	AP 29 '99		
JY 12 '89	DE 12 '0?		
MY 29 '90			
JY 10 '90	NO 0 5 '1?		
JE 25 '91			

© THE BAKER & TAYLOR CO

TYRANNOSAURUS WRECKS
A Book of Dinosaur Riddles

What did the mother and father dinosaur say
when they looked at their dinosaur egg?
"This could be the start of something big!"

by Noelle Sterne   Pictures by Victoria Chess

Thomas Y. Crowell   New York

Why is this dinosaur riddle book dedicated to Jane Sarnoff?
Because her generosity is gigantic.
—*Noelle Sterne*

What does the sign say
at the entrance to a dinosaur cave?
"Home Sweet Stone."

What did the dinosaur say
as he lugged home the groceries?
"Oh, my aching Brachio-saurus!"

How do you tell a
dinosaur to hurry?
"Shake-a-leg-o-saurus."

How does a dinosaur
clean the house?
With a victim cleaner.

What does a dinosaur do
when he needs a rest?
He lies down on his riverbed.

What do you call a dinosaur who
left his armor out in the rain?
A Stegosau-rust.

What kind of cookies
do little dinosaurs like?
Ani-mammal crackers.

What do dinosaurs eat
with their steak?
Marshed potatoes.

What do you call
a dinosaur lollipop?
A prehistor-lick.

What does a dinosaur
put in his cocoa?
Marsh mallows.

Why did the dinosaur
go on a diet?
He weighed too much
for his scales.

What did the mother dinosaur say
when she saw her child's room?
"What a mess-ozoic!"

Who's a dinosaur's favorite babysitter?
Ty-granny-saurus rex.

What did Granny Dino say
to the screaming baby dinosaur?
"You're certainly making a fuss-il!"

Why didn't anyone sleep in the
same room with Daddy dinosaur?
Because he was a Bronto-snorus.

What does a mother dinosaur say
when her child pulls on her tail?
"Honey, don't bog me now."

What are dinosaur children
afraid of at night?
The Boggy Man.

What's a dinosaur's favorite lullaby?
"Rocks-a-bye, baby…"

Why is a dinosaur dangerous at
the wheel of a car?
He's a back-feet driver.

What's the rule when riding in
a carful of dinosaurs?
"Don't jostle the fossils."

Why is a Triceratops
such a nuisance in traffic?
He keeps honking his horns.

What does a dinosaur pay
when she drives over a bridge?
A reptoll.

Why did the Stegosaurus go
to the car repair shop?
So they could fix his broken tail spike.

How does a dinosaur turn down
an invitation to the movies?
"No thanks, I'm not in the mud."

What does the sign say for dinosaurs
waiting to cross the street?
"Don't stalk."

What do you get when dinosaurs
crash their cars?
Tyrannosaurus wrecks.

Where do dinosaurs get
their prescriptions filled?
At the Tyrannosaurus Rexall.

What do you say when
you bump into a dinosaur?
"I bog your pardon."

What made the reptile's car
go off the road?
A flat tire-annosaurus.

What does a dinosaur driver do
before changing lanes on the highway?
He flashes his fern signal.

Why wouldn't you want a dinosaur to help
bring your furniture to your new home?
Because he's probably a slow mover.

What does a dinosaur use
to fix things?
A rep-tool.

What kind of tool does
a reptile carpenter use?
A dino-saw.

How do dinosaur demolition
workers blow up rocks?
With dino-mite.

Who worked on the job
during the fossil holiday?
Just a skeleton crew.

Why did the dinosaur go to the dry cleaner's?
To get his plants pressed.

What kind of reptile makes a good tailor?
A dino-sewer.

What kind of dinosaurs make
good policemen?
Tricera-cops.

How do you direct a dinosaur
to the jungle?
"Go straight ahead,
then take a right fern."

Where does the dinosaur
railroad run?
On the dinosaur tracks.

What do you call a dinosaur cowboy?
Tyrannosaurus Tex.

Who's the Lone Ranger's
favorite dinosaur?
Tonto-saurus.

What kind of dinosaur
does a cowboy ride?
A Bronco-saurus.

Why was the Pentaceratops
a good cattle rancher?
Because he had
a lot of longhorns.

What did the dinosaur
cattle baron say to the outlaw?
"Get off my terror-tory."

What does a dinosaur rustler say
as he makes his getaway?
"Hurry up, let's make tracks!"

How did dinosaurs send letters
in the Old West?
By Bony Express.

How did the dinosaur cowboy feel
after a hard day on the range?
Saddle-saurus.

What do cowboys sing at
roundup on the reptile ranch?
"Git along, little dinos, git along..."

What did the dinosaur senator say
when he looked at a new law?
"Let me chew on this a while."

How did the dinosaur senator
always get his bills passed?
By throwing his weight around.

What do you call a dinosaur
who's elected to Congress?
Rep. Tile.

What do you call the head
of the dinosaur FBI?
Spy-rannosaurus Rex.

What did the dinosaur say when
he thought he had been spied on?
"I think a Bronto-saw-us."

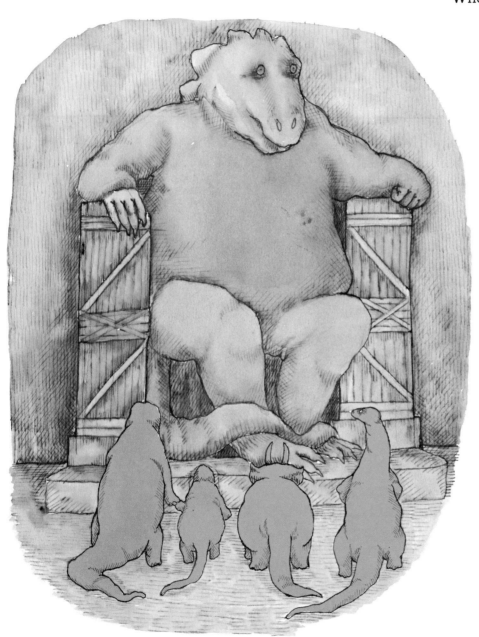

What did the dinosaur Founding Fathers
name their capital city?
Marshington B.C.

What is a famous monument
in the dinosaur capital city?
The Lincoln Mudmorial.

Where was President
Abe Dino born?
In a bog cabin.

What's the last line of the
dinosaur national anthem?
"The land of the tree and
the home of the cave."

What's the dinosaur
national flag?
The Stars and Spikes.

Where do reptiles like to go
for their summer vacation?
   To the dino-shore.

What's a dinosaur's
favorite summer treat?
   An ice-cream stone.

What kind of dinosaur gets
a lot of mosquito bites?
   An Ich-thyosaurus.

Where do dinosaurs
go on hikes?
   In the foss-hills.

What's the weather report
when it's raining dinosaurs?
   Very heavy showers.

What does Santa have for dinosaur children at Christmas?
A big bog full of toys.

What do dinosaurs sing at Christmas?
"Jungle bells, jungle bells…"

What did the little dinosaur want for Christmas?
A toy-rannosaurus rex.

What keeps a dinosaur warm in winter?
A fern-ace.

How does a Pentaceratops celebrate New Year's?
He blows all his horns.

How did the Stegosaurus liven up the party?
She spiked the punch.

What did the dinosaur fossil
say to his friend?
"I haven't seen you for an age!"

Why did the Stegosaurus
wear his spikes to the party?
Because he was a sharp dresser.

What happens when two
dinosaur fossils tell jokes?
They crack each other up.

Why don't dinosaurs
laugh at old jokes?
They're fos-silly.

How do you describe two
dinosaurs talking very seriously?
They're having a
weighty discussion.

Is it all right to ask a dinosaur
lots of questions about the jungle?
Yes, it's one of his favorite
tropics of conversation.

Why do dinosaurs have lots of friends?
Because they're so big-hearted.

What does a dinosaur say to her
sweetheart on Valentine's Day?
"I'm mud about you!"

What do you call two dinosaurs
who have just fallen in love?
Pre-kiss-toric.

How do two dinosaurs in love
walk down the street?
Armor in armor.

What did the dinosaur say when
he hugged his friend?
"I've got a big crush on you."

What do you call a very rich dinosaur?
A gold-blooded reptile.

Where does a dinosaur keep his money?
In a cavings bank.

What do you need to make
a deposit in a cavings bank?
Nickels and dime-osaurs.

What do dinosaurs
pay their bills with?
Tyrannosaurus checks.

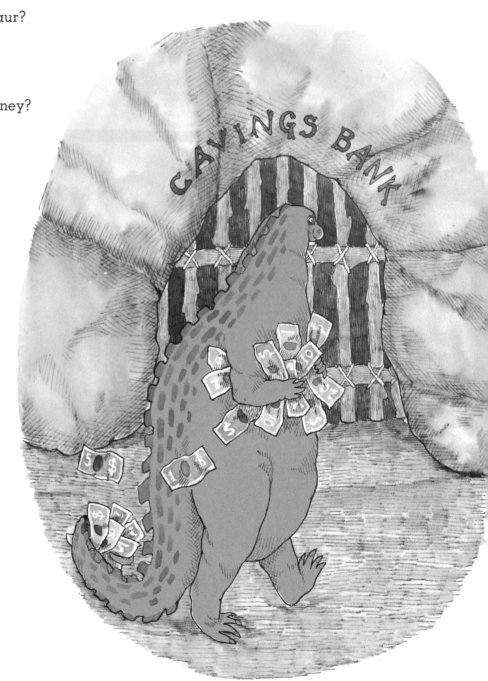

Where does the
dinosaur company president sit?
At his Tyrannosaurus desk.

What did the dinosaur say to his
business partner on the phone?
"I'll coal you in the morning."

What do you call a dinosaur who
types and files in an office?
A secre-terror.

Why do dinosaur executives
take business trips?
To visit the company plants.

When a dinosaur executive travels
by airplane, where does he sit?
In the first grass section.

Why did the dinosaur
gobble up the factory?
Because he was a plant eater.

What do you call a dinosaur telephone?
A rep-dial.

When the rep-dial is out of order,
how does a dinosaur make a call?
On the tele-stone.

How does a dinosaur
send a letter?
Fierce class.

What kind of music
do teen-age dinosaurs like best?
Rocks and roll.

What's a good rhythm
instrument for a dinosaur?
The xylo-stone.

Who's at the keyboard
in the reptile band?
Piano-saurus Rex.

What instrument does
a dinosaur fossil play?
His trom-bone.

What's the latest dance
at the dinosaur disco?
The fossil hustle.

What did the dinosaur
piano teacher tell his student?
"Be sure and practice
your scales."

What did the doctor say
to the sick dinosaur?
"You're looking a little pale-eozoic."

What did the cold-blooded
dinosaur say to the doctor?
"I don't feel so hot."

How do you weigh a dinosaur?
You tip his scales.

What did the doctor say
to the overworked fossil?
"You need to rest
those old bones."

Why did the doctor prescribe
a new diet for the dinosaur fossil?
Because he was
a skeleton of his former self.

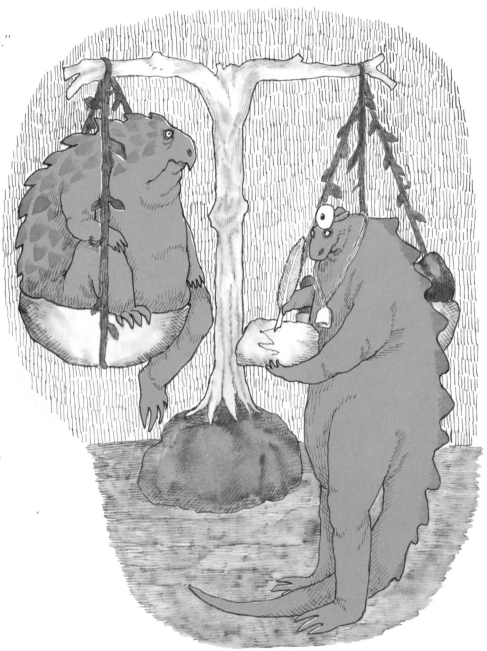

Why was the dinosaur doctor
so popular?
Everyone liked his bogside manner.

What does a dinosaur doctor use
to take temperatures?
A fern-mometer.

How does a dinosaur doctor
check his patient's heart?
He takes his mud pressure.

Where does a dinosaur
study to become a doctor?
Mudical school.

When do you go to see a sick
dinosaur in the hospital?
During visiting horrors.

When a dinosaur has an operation,
where do his relatives stay?
In the wading room.

What do you call a giant dentist
with scaly skin and a long tail?
  An orthodontosaurus.

What do you call a dinosaur
who's late for school?
An overslept-ile.

What does a dinosaur say
when he has a lot of homework?
"I'm swamped!"

What do you call a dinosaur
who's smart in school?
A brain-tosaurus.

How does a dinosaur fossil
get ready for a school test?
He bones up all night.

Why didn't the dinosaur want
to act in the school play?
She got coal feet.

Why did the dinosaur like to play
with his friend?
Because he was tons of fun.

What do you call two dinosaurs
about to burst into giggles?
Pre-hysteric.

What do reptiles like
to play on at the playground?
The dino-see-saw-r.

What do you call
a very quiet dinosaur?
A docile fossil.

What else do you call
a very quiet dinosaur?
Shy-rannosaurus Rex.

Why didn't the dinosaur
want to play with his friends?
He was a stick-in-the-mud.

How do you play dinosaur baseball?
Three spikes and you're out!

Why did the Stegosaurus have
to sit out the rest of the game?
He twisted his armor.

What do you call
a dinosaur cheerleader?
A peptile.

What do you hit the puck
with in dinosaur hockey?
A stick-osaurus.

What did the dinosaur say
when she looked in the mirror?
"Terror, terror on the wall..."

How did the dinosaur princess
find her true love?
She followed the
dinosaur foot-prince.

What did Cinderella Dino
lose at the ball?
Her grass slipper.

What do you call a spell
cast by a dinosaur witch?
A Tyrannosaurus hex.

What was the name of the dinosaur
who called for his fiddlers three?
Old King Coal.

What does Clark Kent-aceratops do when
he wants to change into Super Dino?
He dashes into the nearest stone booth.

How does Super Dino
knock out a criminal?
With dino-might.

How did they build Bionic Dino?
With Pleistocene parts.

Where does a reptile go to buy things?
A dino-store.

What do you call a reptile
who works in a dino-store?
A scalesman.

Why do dino-stores get
a lot of customers?
They're always slashing
their prices.

What did one dinosaur shopper
say to another?
"Your feet are killing me."

What did the dinosaur say
when she bought a new book?
"I can really sink my
teeth into this."

How do you buy dinosaurs?
By the bog-full.

What did the crowd say as the first
flying reptile took off?
"Watch that dino soar!"

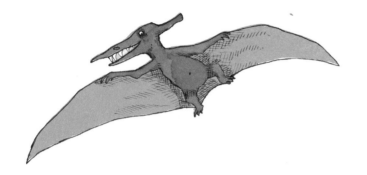

What did the dying dinosaur cry out?
"I'm getting bogged down!"

What did the fossil scientist say to the dinosaur?
"Dig you later."